BRIDGE TECHNIQUE SERIES

PLANNING IN DEFENSE

David Bird • Marc Smith

MASTER POINT PRESS • TORONTO

Master Point Press
331 Douglas Ave
Toronto, Ontario, Canada
M5M 1H2
(416) 781-0351   Internet www.masterpointpress.com

Canadian Cataloguing in Publication Data
Bird, David, 1946-
Planning in defense

(Bridge technique; 11)
ISBN 1-894154-35-5

1. Contract bridge — Defensive play. I. Smith, Marc, 1960-.II. Title. III. Series: Bird, David, 1946-Bridge technique; 11

GV1282.42.B573 2001   795.41'53   C00-933104-2

Cover design and Interior: Olena S. Sullivan
Editor: Ray Lee

Printed and bound in Canada by Webcom Limited

1 2 3 4 5 6 7   07 06 05 04 03 02 01

CONTENTS

Bridge Technique Series

Entry Management

Tricks with Trumps

Safety Plays

Eliminations and Throw-Ins

Deceptive Card Play

Planning in Suit Contracts

Planning in Notrump Contracts

Defensive Signaling

Squeezes made Simple

Planning in Defense

Reading the Cards

Tricks with Finesses

Signals and Discards

....

When you start playing with a new partner, it is important to agree what type of signals and discards you will use. Otherwise you will have little chance of defending to maximum effect. In the same way, when you set out to write a book on defense, it is a good idea to state at the outset which types of signals and discards will be assumed. Let's do it!

Signaling in defense

In our earlier book in this series, *Signaling in Defense*, we recommended that an opening lead of the ace or queen should ask partner to give an attitude signal (high to encourage, low to discourage). A lead of the king should request a count signal (high to show an even number of cards in the suit, low to show an odd number). In all other situations, we recommended that the defenders should signal their count. Why was that?

Apart from the fact that it enables the defenders to build a quick picture of the whole deal, there are many single suit situations where a count signal can help. Suppose you are West, defending 3NT, and you lead a fourth-best heart here:

....

♡ Q J 5

♡ K 10 7 4 3 ♡ 9 8 2

♡ A 6

Dummy's queen wins the first round and declarer attacks some other suit, allowing you to regain the lead. Should you play another heart now? If South's ace is bare, that will work well. If the ace is still guarded, a heart continuation will give away a trick. The only way you can read the position is for your partner to signal his length on the first round. Here he would play the two, advertising a three-card holding. As this leaves declarer with only two hearts, you would continue the suit. If instead East had started with ♡9-2, he would signal with the nine on the first round. Warned that declarer held three cards in hearts, you would try a different suit when you gained the lead.

Discarding

What is the best discard system to play? Some players like Lavinthal or McKenney discards — where you throw a high card to suggest a switch to the higher of the other two suits, a low card to suggest a switch to the lower suit. We are not great admirers of this method. Those who use it often take each discard as a command to switch somewhere, even when the defender making the discard has no great wish for any particular play. 'You did ask for a club,' is the usual wail as yet another contract is let through!

When you try to help partner, with a signal or a discard, you should aim to describe your hand rather than to tell him what to do. How, indeed, can you know what is the best line of defense when you can see only your own cards and not partner's? It is better to describe your own hand, then leave it to partner to work out what is best.

We recommend a simple system of discarding — 'keep winners, throw losers!' In general, you will throw from a suit in which you have no interest. A high card will show an even number of cards in the suit, a low card an odd number.

Perhaps your reaction is: 'I can't be bothered with all these count signals and discards. I play bridge for enjoyment.' That's fine by us. It's your choice! But you will never be able to defend with consistent accuracy. Too many times you will have to guess what to do and that is something that top players hate.

CHAPTER • 2

Opening Leads

....

'It all depends on the lead you get.' How often have you heard someone say that? The defenders have relatively few chances to affect the outcome of a contract, particularly a high-level one, and it is vital to make the most telling strike at Trick 1. We will look first at the opening lead against notrump, then move to the more varied options available when leading against a suit contract.

THE OPENING LEAD AGAINST NOTRUMP

The best attack against a notrump contract is usually the suit that is most strongly held by the defenders. If you have a good suit of your own, and it has not been bid by the opponents, you need look no further. Otherwise you may have to judge from the opponents' bidding whether partner may have a good suit for you to attack

Which suit should I lead?

Suppose the bidding has been an unhelpful 1NT-3NT and you have to find a lead from this hand:

♠ K J 8 2 ♡ J 7 3 ◇ K 7 6 2 ♣ 8 4

You would lead a spade rather than a diamond. There are two reasons for this. Firstly, spades is a major suit; if the dummy held four spades, he might well have bid Stayman. The second reason is that you have the jack of spades backing up the king. Leading from an honor gives away about half a trick, on average. The chance of giving away a trick is reduced when you have a second card, such as the jack or ten, backing the top honor.

What would you lead from this hand, after 1NT-3NT?

♠ 9 4　♡ 10 9 3　◇ Q 7 6 2　♣ K 6 5 2

Here neither of the minor-suit honors has any backing. You are quite likely to give away a trick by attacking in either of these suits. The risk would be worthwhile if you held a five-card suit, because there would be a greater prospect of establishing long cards in the suit. With only four-card holdings in the minors, most top players would choose a heart lead (the ♡10). This is unlikely to give away a trick and may strike a good suit in partner's hand.

When the opponents stop in 2NT, or reach 3NT via a limited auction such as 1NT-2NT-3NT, it is particularly important to avoid conceding a cheap trick with the opening lead. Suppose, after such an auction, you must choose a lead from:

♠ 9 8 4　♡ K 10 6 2　◇ A Q 8 3　♣ 10 3

Had the auction been 1NT-3NT, you would lead a heart. Declarer might have values to spare and you must hope to establish some tricks for your side. Against a limited auction it is wiser to lead a spade, aiming to give nothing away. Let declarer work for his tricks.

Now suppose that the opponents have bid 1◇-1♠-2NT-3NT and you must find a lead from:

♠ A J 8 2　♡ 8 2　◇ K 9 8 4　♣ J 8 3

With both your four-card suits bid against you, the choice is between a heart and a club. A doubleton is rarely an inviting lead, unless partner has bid the suit. Reach for the ♣3.

Which card should I lead?

Once you have decided which suit to lead, the choice of card is a matter of convention. Unless you hold three or more honors, including at least two touching honors, this is the scheme:

- Lead the fourth-best card from a holding with one or more honors (the four from K-J-9-4-2).

- Lead the top card from a doubleton, also from holdings such as Q-J-3 or J-10-4.

- Lead the bottom card from honor third (the six from Q-9-6).

- Otherwise lead the second-best card (the seven from 8-7-5-2, the six from 9-6-3).

How can you read the lead of a middle card such as the six or seven? By recalling the bidding and inspecting the other cards on view, you will usually be able to tell whether partner is leading from a strong suit or a weak suit.

Suppose, after bidding of 1NT-3NT, partner attacks this suit:

Partner leads the ♠7 and we'll suppose first that declarer plays the queen from dummy. Even if the bidding does not exclude a holding of A-J-9-7 with West, you should reason that declarer would have played the 10 from dummy if he held two low spades in his hand. You should therefore withhold the king, signaling count with the six.

Suppose instead that declarer calls for the ten from dummy at Trick 1. Now he is destined to make a trick even if partner has led from A-J-9-7. Again there is nothing to be gained, and plenty to be lost, by playing the king. Most of the time it will be clear from the bidding if the lead is from 9-7-x-x and that declarer holds A-J doubleton.

When you hold a three-honor combination including two touching honors, you should usually lead the higher of the touching honors. So, you lead the jack from K-J-10-x, the ten from Q-10-9-x-x. These holdings are known as 'interior sequences'.

From 'broken sequences' such as to A-K-J-x-x or K-Q-10-9-x, you choose which honor to lead according to the signal you would like partner to give. This is the scheme:

- The lead of an ace or queen asks for an attitude signal.
- The lead of a king asks for an unblock, otherwise a count signal.

We dealt fully with this subject in *Signaling in Defense*.

Here are a few examples:

◇ 9 7

◇ A K J 10 3   ◇ 8 6 2

◇ Q 5 4

You lead the king of diamonds against 3NT, requesting the unblock of any honor, otherwise a count signal. When partner follows with the two you know (a) that he does not hold the queen and (b) that he holds three diamonds. South's queen must therefore be guarded. If you held a certain entry in some other side suit, you might choose to clear the diamonds next. Otherwise, you would seek an entry to partner's hand, so he could play a diamond through declarer's queen.

◇ 9 7

◇ A K J 10 3   ◇ 8 6 5 2

◇ Q 4

This time the king draws the six from East and the four from South. Holding four cards, East would signal with the second-best card (followed by the third-best), so you know it is possible that South's queen is doubleton. Furthermore, if East holds two diamonds to South's four, one lead through the queen will not be enough to bring in the suit, even if you could put partner on lead. It will usually be best to continue with the diamond ace, hoping to drop the queen from South.

THE OPENING LEAD AGAINST A SUIT CONTRACT

The best attack against a suit contract is more difficult to determine. These are the main options:

- Lead an unbid side suit, with the aim of cashing or establishing tricks there.

- Lead a short suit — a singleton or doubleton — in the hope of obtaining a ruff.

- Lead a trump, hoping to reduce declarer's ruffing potential.

Once you have decided which suit to lead, there is little problem in choosing the particular card. The conventional choice is the same as in notrump, with these two exceptions. Firstly, do *not* underlead an ace. Except against contracts at the five-level or higher, it is generally a poor idea to lead from a suit containing an ace not accompanied by the king. If you do decide to lead from a holding such as A-8-4-2, lead the ace, not a low card. The second exception is that from a four-card or longer holding headed by touching honors, lead the top honor rather than a low card. For example, you would lead the king from K-Q-6-2, the queen from Q-J-7-5-3. The third round of the suit will doubtless be ruffed by someone or other. It is essential that your honors play a role on the first two rounds.

We will look more closely now at the three types of lead against a suit contract.

Leading an unbid side suit

This is the type of lead that we like best. Suppose the opponents' bidding has gone 1♠-2◇-2♠-4♠. There is a fair chance that declarer's plan will be to draw trumps, establish the diamonds, then throw his losers away on the long cards in diamond suit. You cannot afford to waste any time! Attack in one of the unbid suits, aiming to cash — or at least establish — whatever winners you may have there.

Layouts such as the following are dealt by the million:

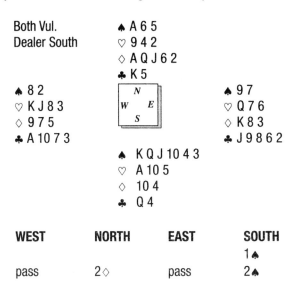

	♠ A 6 5		
Both Vul.	♡ 9 4 2		
Dealer South	◇ A Q J 6 2		
	♣ K 5		
♠ 8 2			♠ 9 7
♡ K J 8 3			♡ Q 7 6
◇ 9 7 5			◇ K 8 3
♣ A 10 7 3			♣ J 9 8 6 2
	♠ K Q J 10 4 3		
	♡ A 10 5		
	◇ 10 4		
	♣ Q 4		

WEST	NORTH	EAST	SOUTH
			1♠
pass	2◇	pass	2♠
pass	4♠	all pass	

It is essential that you attack in either hearts or clubs. Since leading a suit containing the ace without the king is rarely a good idea, you should have no hesitation in reaching for the ♡3. On this occasion you are lucky. Partner obliges with the queen and, when the diamond finesse fails, you will have four tricks to take.

What if declarer had held the ♡Q instead of your partner? Your lead would then have cost nothing. Declarer would have set up the diamonds anyway.

There is only one word to describe those who say that they 'don't like to lead away from a king' in such circumstances. Losers! Finish ahead of them, next time you play, by being willing to attack such suits.

Leading a short suit

A singleton in an unbid suit is nearly always a promising lead. Provided you hold at least two trumps, you will score a ruff when partner holds either the ace of the suit you have led or the trump ace. A singleton in a suit that the opponents have bid is not so promising. Even if you score a ruff, you may find that you have helped to set up declarer's winners. He may now be able to discard losers in some other suit where you would otherwise have scored a trick or two.

What about doubleton leads? We are not great admirers of them. You are that bit further away from your ruff and declarer will often be able to draw trumps before partner has the chance to give you a ruff. Particularly risky is the lead of a doubleton honor. You are too likely to run into this sort of scenario:

```
                 ◇ Q 8 3
              ┌───────────┐
              │     N     │
   ◇ J 5      │  W     E  │      ◇ K 9 7 6 2
              │     S     │
              └───────────┘
                 ◇ A 10 4
```

The first round goes jack, queen, king and ace. Partner will not even be able to continue the suit safely, should he gain the lead. Left to himself, with this holding, declarer might have played low to the queen and king, followed by a finesse of the ten! So, fire away with your singletons but lead a doubleton only as a last resort.

One final point is that the odds on any type of short-suit lead improve when you hold a top trump. You will then have the opportunity to cross to partner's hand when you gain the lead in the trump suit.

Leading a trump

What is our general opinion on trump leads? They are overrated! You should certainly not lead a trump as a result of the ancient ditty 'When in doubt, lead a trump.' Prefer instead: 'When in doubt, lead an unbid side suit.'

Nevertheless, there are a few standard situations when a trump lead is likely to prove effective:

When responder has given preference to the opener's second suit. After an auction such as 1♠-1NT-2♡-pass, you can expect responder to hold something like one spade and three hearts. A trump lead may cut down declarer's spade ruffs.

When greatly outgunned opponents have taken a high-level sacrifice. If you and your partner hold 27 points between you and the opponents have sacrificed in 5♣ over your spade game, you can be sure they are expecting to make quite a few trump tricks. A trump lead may reduce these.

When partner passes out a low-level takeout double (in an auction such as 1◇-dbl-all pass), he is likely to hold excellent trumps. He is expecting you to lead a trump — if you have one — so that he can draw declarer's trumps.

Apart from these situations our advice is to lead trumps sparingly.

Leading against suit slams

The opening lead is rarely more critical than at the slam level. You will gain the lead only once more, at most, so it is essential to make the most of your opportunity at Trick 1. Our general advice against a small slam in a suit is: attack! If you make a passive lead, such as a trump, the opponents will generally have the power to amass twelve tricks.

Suppose the opponents have bid diamonds and clubs and you must find a lead against 6◇ from this hand:

♠ K 10 8 3   ♡ J 8 3 2   ◇ 10 9 2   ♣ A 5

Lead the ♠3! You hope that partner can produce the queen and you will be able to cash a spade trick when you come on lead with the ace of clubs. A heart lead may be right, but it is much less likely — even if you find partner with the king or queen, declarer may still have double protection in the suit.

What if you hold this hand, again leading against the same 6♢ contract?

♠ K 10 8 3   ♡ A 8 3 2   ♢ 10 9 2   ♣ 9 5

Players debate for hours on the question 'Should you lead an ace against a slam?' Leading the ♡A will certainly work well if partner holds the ♡K and the declarer has two quick losers in the suit. This is unlikely, however, particularly if the opponents are competent bidders. As neither opponent has bid hearts, it is also unlikely that partner will be able to ruff the second round.

We favor a spade lead. For every hundred times an ace lead is successful against a slam, you will find two hundred cases where it gives the slam away. However, the situation is much closer if you are playing matchpoints, when simply cashing your ace to save the overtrick may be worth a great deal.

Is a singleton a good lead against a slam? Suppose the opponents bid spades and clubs on their way to 6♠. What would you lead from:

♠ 9 6 3   ♡ 4   ♢ J 10 8 7 3   ♣ A 9 5 2

Since you hold an ace in your own hand and the opponents are in a slam, you cannot expect your partner to hold an ace. The singleton heart would therefore be a poor lead — it is much too likely to give away partner's holding in the suit. You should lead the ♢J instead.

Suppose now that your ♣A was the ♣Q instead. Now you wouldn't think twice before leading the singleton. If partner were to hold either of the major-suit aces, you would very likely score the setting trick with a heart ruff.

What sort of lead should you seek against a grand slam in a suit? There is absolutely no point in trying to set up a trick with your lead — if you get in to cash it declarer will be one down anyway. So, you should seek a safe lead. A trump will often be safest but remember that a singleton trump is a dangerous choice. If partner has a holding such as Q-x-x or J-x-x-x in the suit, you will owe him a drink!

Leading against notrump slams

It is truly amazing how many players choose exactly the same lead against 6NT as they would have done against 3NT. When you lead a club from K-10-x-x-x against 3NT you do so in the knowledge that the lead may cost a trick in the suit. You are happy to take this risk because there is a good chance that you can establish some long cards. When you are on lead against 6NT you cannot afford to give away a trick! Doing so is almost certain to allow the slam to make.

Against 6NT, you should look for a safe lead. In general, lead from the longest suit in which you do not hold an honor. Suppose, after bidding of 2NT-6NT, that you have to find a lead from:

♠ J942   ♡ 8752   ◇ K73   ♣ 92

A heart lead is safest and therefore best. A club lead would be next safest. To lead either a spade or a diamond would be a serious mistake — all too likely to give away a critical trick.

Key points

1. When leading against notrump games and part scores, generally lead the longest suit that has not been bid by the opponents. When you are long in the opponents' suits, look for an unbid suit that partner may hold.

2. Unless you have some sort of honor sequence, lead fourth best from a suit containing an honor. Lead the second best card from a suit without an honor.

3. Lead the top of touching cards from an internal sequence (the jack from K-J-10). Lead the top card from a doubleton or from holdings such as Q-J-x or J-10-x. From honor third, lead the lowest card (the three from K-6-3).

4. When you lead from an A-K against a suit contract lead 'ace for attitude, king for count', according to which signal you would like your partner to give.

5. A king lead against notrumps asks for 'unblock or count'. You would make such a lead from A-K-J-10-x, expecting partner to unblock the queen if he held it (otherwise to give count).

6. The best idea, generally, against a suit contract is to attack in an unbid suit. A side-suit singleton is also a promising lead. Doubleton leads are less attractive. Trump leads are right in certain circumstances but should not be a general fall-back because you do not have any brighter ideas!

QUIZ

A.   ♠ A Q 7 4   ♡ J 8 3   ◇ 10 9 2   ♣ K 6 4

WEST	NORTH	EAST	SOUTH
			1NT
pass	3NT	all pass	

Rank an opening lead in each of the four suits in order of preference, from best to worst. (For example: spades first, hearts second, etc.) Would you answer this question differently if the bidding had gone 1NT-2NT-pass?

B.   ♠ K J 8 2   ♡ J 4   ◇ A K 8 3   ♣ 10 6 4

WEST	NORTH	EAST	SOUTH
			1NT
pass	3NT	all pass	

Rank an opening lead in each of the four suits in order of preference.

C.   ♠ A 2   ♡ K 8 7 5 3   ◇ J 5 3   ♣ 9 8 4

WEST	NORTH	EAST	SOUTH
			1◇
pass	1♡	pass	1NT
pass	3NT	all pass	

Rank an opening lead in each of the four suits in order of preference.

D.   ♠ 10 9 3   ♡ 10 6 4   ◇ J 2   ♣ Q 10 7 6 2

WEST	NORTH	EAST	SOUTH
			1NT
pass	3NT	all pass	

Rank an opening lead in each of the four suits in order of preference

E.   ♠ 8 7 4   ♡ Q 10 8 3   ◇ J 9 5 2   ♣ Q 4

Rank an opening lead in each of the four suits in order of preference.

WEST	NORTH	EAST	SOUTH
			1♠
pass	2◇	pass	2♠
pass	4♠	all pass	

F.   ♠ 5   ♡ A 4 2   ◇ A K J 8 4 3   ♣ J 6 4 2

Rank an opening lead in each of the four suits in order of preference.

WEST	NORTH	EAST	SOUTH
			1♡
2◇	2♡	3◇	4♡
all pass			

G.   ♠ Q 10 6 4   ♡ K 4   ◇ 10 5 3   ♣ A 9 6 2

Rank an opening lead in each of the four suits in order of preference.

WEST	NORTH	EAST	SOUTH
			1♡
pass	1NT	pass	2◇
all pass			

H.   ♠ K 9 7 3   ♡ 10 6 4   ◇ A 2   ♣ 10 9 8 2

WEST	NORTH	EAST	SOUTH
	1♣	pass	2♡
pass	3♡	pass	4NT
pass	5♡	pass	6♡
all pass			

Rank an opening lead in each of the four suits in order of preference.

Answers

A. (1) ♠4 (2) ◇10 (3) ♣4 (4) ♡3. Leads of the ♠4 (attacking) and the ◇10 (passive) are roughly equal in merit. Remember that you will give away half a trick — on average — by leading a spade. Nevertheless you may find partner with something useful, such as the jack, thereby setting up tricks in the suit. A club is slightly better than a heart. Both leads risk conceding a trick but in clubs you have more chance of setting up some tricks your way. Against a limited auction such as 1NT-2NT, you would prefer a diamond lead to a spade lead.

B. (1) ◇A (2) ♠2 (3) ♣4 (4) ♡J. A low spade is much better than a low diamond. However, the best idea is to lead the ◇A, to look at dummy and see which attitude signal partner gives you.

C. (1) ♣8 (2) ◇3 (3) ♡5 (4) ♠A. A heart lead is not a good idea when dummy has bid the suit. A club is better than a diamond because it is less likely to give away a trick.

D. (1) ♠10 (2) ♡4 (3) ♣6 (4) ◇J. There is little point in leading a club because you have no entry to enjoy the long cards, even if you can set up the suit. Indeed, the lack of a Stayman bid from North suggests that partner will be very short in clubs. A spade, from your sequence, is marginally better than a heart from the unsupported ten.

E. (1) ♡3 (2) ♣Q (3) ♠4 (4) ◇2. It is easily best to lead a heart, hoping to set up some tricks there before declarer gets dummy's diamonds going. Remember that leading from a doubleton is much less attractive than leading a singleton. A club lead is also more likely to give a trick away.

F. (1) ♠5 (2) ◇K (3) ♣2 (4) ♡A. It is easily best to lead your singleton spade. When you gain the lead with the ♡A you will have the chance to underlead your ◇AK to put partner on lead with the queen (you hope!) He will then be able to deliver a spade ruff. If you cash a top diamond first, this will not be possible. Either dummy or declarer is almost certain to hold a singleton diamond.

G. (1) ◇3 (2) ♠4 (3) ♣A (4) ♡K. This is an auction that cries out for a trump lead. The most likely red-suit shape for North is one heart and three diamonds. You should therefore lead a trump to cut down declarer's ruffs. A spade lead is much better than a club, because it is rarely right to lead from an ace unsupported by the king.

H. (1) ♠3 (2) ◇A (3) ♡4 (4) ♣2. It is unlikely that South has bid Blackwood with two top losers in diamonds (even if he has, his partner may hold the diamond king). A spade lead is much better than a diamond because if you find partner with the queen you may set up a second trick for the defense. A club lead is worse than a trump because you may assist declarer in his play of dummy's main suit.

CHAPTER 3

Basic Defense at Notrump

In this chapter, we will look at the most important techniques available when defending against a notrump contract. Single suit situations, which occur in a suit contract as well as in notrump, are covered in the next chapter.

Maintaining communications

To beat a 3NT contract, the defenders usually have to set up some long cards in their best combined suit. To be able to score these long cards they may need to preserve communications between the hands. This can be done to maximum advantage only if the defenders can tell how the suit lies. Look at this situation:

$$\diamond\ 8\ 4$$

```
        N
    W       E
        S
```

$$\diamond\ K\ 10\ 7\ 6\ 3 \qquad\qquad \diamond\ A\ 9\ 2$$

$$\diamond\ Q\ J\ 5$$

Sitting West, you lead the ◇6 to partner's ace. He returns another diamond and South plays the queen. Suppose you have no outside entry and expect partner to gain the lead next. Should you win the trick, do you think, or hold up the king? You cannot answer this question unless you are told which diamond your partner returned at Trick 2. By his choice of card your partner will tell you how many diamonds he holds. With two cards remaining, he will return the higher card. With three or more cards, he will generally return his original fourth-best card.

Here East has two cards remaining and will return the nine. This tells you that declarer started with Q-J-5. You should hold up the king so that partner will have an easy entry to your hand if he gains the lead later. (If South started with Q-J-5-2, and was clever enough to play the five on the first round, it is unlikely you can beat the contract).

Let's look at a full deal where it is essential for West to play correctly at Trick 2.

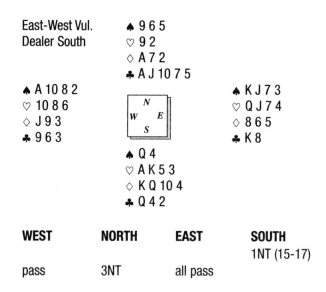

```
East-West Vul.        ♠ 9 6 5
Dealer South          ♡ 9 2
                      ◇ A 7 2
                      ♣ A J 10 7 5
   ♠ A 10 8 2                          ♠ K J 7 3
   ♡ 10 8 6            ┌──────┐        ♡ Q J 7 4
   ◇ J 9 3             │  N   │        ◇ 8 6 5
   ♣ 9 6 3            W│      │E        ♣ K 8
                      │  S   │
                      └──────┘
                      ♠ Q 4
                      ♡ A K 5 3
                      ◇ K Q 10 4
                      ♣ Q 4 2
```

WEST	NORTH	EAST	SOUTH
			1NT (15-17)
pass	3NT	all pass	

You lead the ♠2 against 3NT and partner wins with the king. He returns the ♠3 and South produces the queen. Since you have no outside entry to your hand, it would be right to hold up the ace if declarer had started with ♠Q-J-4. By doing so, you would retain an entry to your hand, allowing partner to cross over when he gained the lead. On this deal, however, South cannot possibly hold ♠Q-J-4. This would leave East with an initial holding of ♠K-7-3. He would then have returned the seven on the second round instead of the three.

Since a hold-up cannot be productive, you should win the second round of spades and continue with the ♠10. Declarer holds only two spades so you will score four spade tricks. When the club finesse loses, the game will go one down. You may be thinking: 'what if declarer held four spades and partner's ♠3 return was from ♠K-3?' In that case your play has cost nothing. By returning the ten on the third round, you have at least stopped declarer from scoring two tricks in the suit.

When partner leads a suit that you have bid, you may need to play carefully in the third seat. Again your aim is to preserve communications.

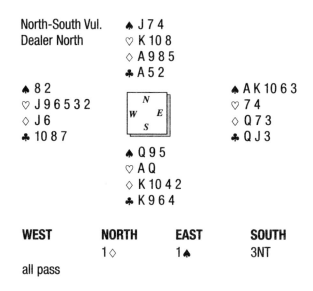

North-South Vul.
Dealer North

♠ J 7 4
♡ K 10 8
◇ A 9 8 5
♣ A 5 2

♠ 8 2
♡ J 9 6 5 3 2
◇ J 6
♣ 10 8 7

♠ A K 10 6 3
♡ 7 4
◇ Q 7 3
♣ Q J 3

♠ Q 9 5
♡ A Q
◇ K 10 4 2
♣ K 9 6 4

WEST	NORTH	EAST	SOUTH
	1◇	1♠	3NT
all pass			

In response to your overcall, West leads the ♠8 against 3NT. How will you defend when declarer plays the jack from dummy?

If you capture the first round of spades, declarer will make his contract. It will do you no good to clear the spade suit because he will duck a diamond into the safe (West) hand. Partner cannot put you on lead to score the long spades and declarer will have nine tricks.

See the difference if you allow dummy's jack to win. Declarer has only eight tricks. Whichever defender gains the lead in diamonds, the communications will be intact to enjoy four spade winners.

There is no point worrying that declarer may hold ♠Q-9-x-x. So he may, but in that case he is sure to score two spade tricks anyway and there is very little prospect of beating the contract.

Clearing the suit you have led

You lead your longest suit and partner brings a smile to your lips by winning with a big card. The work may not be over. You will sometimes have to overtake partner's next card to ensure defeat of the contract. Suppose you are defending 3NT and you lead the ♡6 in this situation:

♡ 9 7 3

♡ Q 10 8 6   W   E   ♡ A J

♡ K 5 4 2

    Partner wins with the ace and returns the ♡J, declarer playing low. This is not the moment to sit back, congratulating yourself on your choice of lead. Partner may have only two hearts! You must overtake with the queen and return the ♡10, pinning dummy's nine. If instead you fail to overtake, partner will have to switch elsewhere and your side may end with two heart tricks instead of three.

    When you have a quick entry in another suit it is often right to overtake, even though this will give declarer a trick in the suit. Look at this deal:

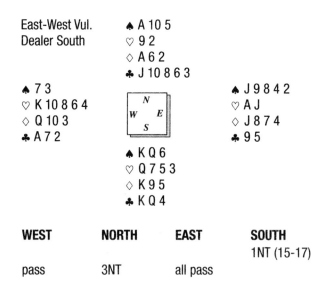

East-West Vul.
Dealer South

♠ A 10 5
♡ 9 2
◇ A 6 2
♣ J 10 8 6 3

♠ 7 3
♡ K 10 8 6 4
◇ Q 10 3
♣ A 7 2

♠ J 9 8 4 2
♡ A J
◇ J 8 7 4
♣ 9 5

♠ K Q 6
♡ Q 7 5 3
◇ K 9 5
♣ K Q 4

WEST	NORTH	EAST	SOUTH
			1NT (15-17)
pass	3NT	all pass	

    The opponents reach 3NT and you lead the ♡6. Partner wins with the ace and returns the ♡J, declarer playing low. What now?

If partner has another heart you will be able to take five heart tricks and the ace of clubs, putting the game two down. However, partner may hold only two hearts. To make sure of defeating the game, you should overtake the jack of hearts with the king and then lead the ♡ 10 to clear the suit. Declarer cannot come close to nine tricks without playing on clubs. You will pounce with the ace and cash two hearts to break the game.

Clearing the suit partner has led

When declarer has two stoppers to knock out before he can claim nine tricks in 3NT, the defenders may have to take these stoppers at the right moment. Hands such as the following are dealt by the bushel:

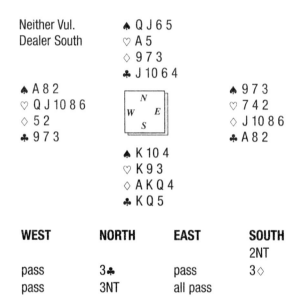

```
Neither Vul.          ♠ Q J 6 5
Dealer South          ♡ A 5
                      ◇ 9 7 3
                      ♣ J 10 6 4
 ♠ A 8 2                               ♠ 9 7 3
 ♡ Q J 10 8 6          N               ♡ 7 4 2
 ◇ 5 2            W         E          ◇ J 10 8 6
 ♣ 9 7 3               S               ♣ A 8 2
                      ♠ K 10 4
                      ♡ K 9 3
                      ◇ A K Q 4
                      ♣ K Q 5
```

WEST	NORTH	EAST	SOUTH
			2NT
pass	3♣	pass	3◇
pass	3NT	all pass	

Take the East cards. Your partner leads the queen of hearts and this card is allowed to win. Although it does not matter much on this particular deal, you should signal with the ♡2 to show an odd number of cards in the suit. Declarer wins the second round of hearts with dummy's ace and plays the jack of clubs. What should you do?

You should fly in with the ace and return your last heart, clearing partner's suit. The contract will now go down. Diamonds do not break 3-3 and, when declarer plays on spades, partner will win and cash two hearts to put the contract one down.

Suppose instead that you see no hurry to rise with the club ace. Declarer will pocket one club trick, then switch to spades. Three spade tricks will bring his total to nine and the contract will be made. Rising with the club ace would be right too if partner held the club king. Again you would take your winner first and clear partner's suit. Partner could then score the long cards when his stopper was knocked out.

Reading the opening lead

When you play the method 'fourth best from good suits, second best from bad suits', it is usually easy for the defender in third seat to read the position. This is particularly so when the opponents have bid a suit or two and you already have some idea of the distribution.

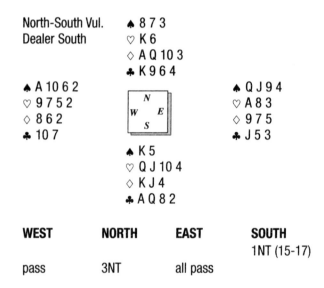

	North-South Vul.		♠ 8 7 3	
	Dealer South		♡ K 6	
			◇ A Q 10 3	
			♣ K 9 6 4	

♠ A 10 6 2		♠ Q J 9 4
♡ 9 7 5 2		♡ A 8 3
◇ 8 6 2		◇ 9 7 5
♣ 10 7		♣ J 5 3

		♠ K 5	
		♡ Q J 10 4	
		◇ K J 4	
		♣ A Q 8 2	

WEST	NORTH	EAST	SOUTH
			1NT (15-17)
pass	3NT	all pass	

After uninformative bidding by the opponents, your partner leads the ♡7 against 3NT. The king is played from the dummy and you win with the ace. What now?

Many players would have their ♡8 on the table without even pausing to think. However, there was a message hidden in your partner's ♡7 lead. Either it was a second-best card from small cards, or it was fourth-best from an honor holding. What honor holding could West have? If he held Q-10-9-7-2 he would have led the ten. With J-10-9-7-2 he would have led the jack and with Q-J-9-7-2 he would have led the queen. So, you can be fairly sure, once you stop to think, that declarer holds the missing honors in the heart suit. Having come to this conclusion, it is not too difficult to find the spade switch. Four further tricks roll in and the game is defeated.

Suppose, on this deal, that declarer tries to be clever— dropping the jack on the first round of hearts to suggest that he is short in the suit. You will not be deceived by this. If declarer did indeed start with queen-jack doubleton, your partner would be left with ♡10-9-7-5-4-2. He would not have led the seven, would he? He would have led a fourth-best ♡5. Again you should switch to the spade queen.

On the next deal you can tell from partner's fourth-best lead that declarer has a strong holding in the suit led:

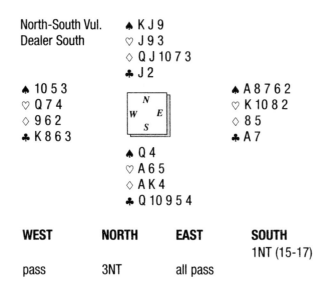

North-South Vul.	♠ K J 9		
Dealer South	♡ J 9 3		
	◊ Q J 10 7 3		
	♣ J 2		

♠ 10 5 3		♠ A 8 7 6 2
♡ Q 7 4		♡ K 10 8 2
◊ 9 6 2		◊ 8 5
♣ K 8 6 3		♣ A 7

	♠ Q 4	
	♡ A 6 5	
	◊ A K 4	
	♣ Q 10 9 5 4	

WEST	NORTH	EAST	SOUTH
			1NT (15-17)
pass	3NT	all pass	

Partner leads the ♣3 and you capture dummy's jack with the ace. What now?

How many clubs does partner hold? Four, yes, because his fourth-best card was the three and you can see the two in dummy. That leaves declarer with a five-card club holding. The fact that he saw fit to 'waste' dummy's jack on the first trick confirms that South's club holding is a strong one. If you return a second club the contract will easily be made. Declarer will score five diamonds, three clubs, and the ace of hearts — at least. Instead you should switch to a low heart, hoping to find partner with the queen. When this comes to pass, you will score three hearts, two clubs and a spade, putting the game two down.

Suppose, on that deal, the club suit had been slightly different:

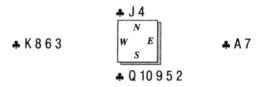

♣ J 4

♣ K 8 6 3   N / W E / S   ♣ A 7

♣ Q 10 9 5 2

Again partner leads the ♣3 to your ace (whether or not declarer chose to play dummy's jack). A cunning South may follow with the five, hoping to make it look as if West holds five clubs. It may still be worthwhile considering a switch. You know that declarer holds at least four clubs and that a continuation of the suit may be unproductive.

Reading partner's return

Sometimes you are unlucky with your opening lead and strike a suit where declarer is well protected. Provided you can read partner's holding, it may not be too late to switch elsewhere.

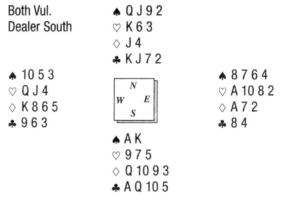

Both Vul.   ♠ Q J 9 2
Dealer South   ♡ K 6 3
                  ◇ J 4
                  ♣ K J 7 2

♠ 10 5 3   ♠ 8 7 6 4
♡ Q J 4   ♡ A 10 8 2
◇ K 8 6 5   ◇ A 7 2
♣ 9 6 3   ♣ 8 4

                  ♠ A K
                  ♡ 9 7 5
                  ◇ Q 10 9 3
                  ♣ A Q 10 5

WEST	NORTH	EAST	SOUTH
			1NT (15-17)
pass	2♣	pass	2◇
pass	3NT	all pass	

You lead the ◇5 against 3NT. The jack is played from dummy and your partner wins with the ace, declarer dropping the three. When the ◇7 is returned, declarer plays the queen and you must decide how to proceed.

Partner has returned the seven and you have not yet seen the two. So, one possibility is that partner started with A-7-2. Could the ◇7 possibly be a fourth-best card? If South started with ◇Q-3, East would hold ◇A-10-9-7-2. Knowing from your lead that you held an honor, he would surely have returned the ten to expose the position.

In any case it is long odds against South holding a doubleton diamond when he has denied four cards in either major. You should read South for four diamonds, including the two masters in the suit. In this case a heart switch seems to be the best prospect. Partner produces the required A-10-x-x and another contract bites the dust.

On many hands, including this one, it was not 100% clear whether to continue your suit or switch elsewhere. Give the matter some thought, considering all the spot cards you have seen, and you will make the right decision more often than not.

Avoiding a blockage

One of the saddest ways to lose points is to block a suit and not be able to cash the winners that were your due. Look at this deal:

```
East-West Vul.        ♠  10 5
Dealer South          ♡  A Q J 5
                      ◇  10 9 8 2
                      ♣  K 7 2

♠ Q J 8 3                              ♠ K 9 7 4 2
♡ 10 7 6             ┌─────────┐       ♡ 8 4 2
◇ 7 6 4             │    N    │        ◇ A 3
♣ J 6 5             │ W     E │        ♣ Q 9 4
                    │    S    │
                     └─────────┘
                      ♠  A 6
                      ♡  K 9 3
                      ◇  K Q J 5
                      ♣  A 10 8 3
```

WEST	NORTH	EAST	SOUTH
			1NT (15-17)
pass	2♣	pass	2◇
pass	3NT	all pass	

West led the ♠3 to East's king and declarer allowed this card to win. When the ♠4 was returned, declarer won with the ace and West followed with the eight, mentally recording that his queen and jack were now good. Declarer had little option but to play on diamonds and East gained the lead with the ace. Much good did it do him! When he returned a spade West claimed two tricks in the suit and East's remaining spade winner withered on the vine.

West should have unblocked the queen of spades on the second round, retaining ♠J-8. When East gained the lead in diamonds and returned a third round of spades, West could win with the jack and return the ♠8 for East to overtake with the nine. The defenders would then have scored four spades and one diamond, beating the game.

On this particular deal there was no excuse for West's carelessness. South's Stayman response had denied four spades so there could be no possible need to retain both the queen and the jack.

When to break the 'rules'

You cannot become a top class bridge player merely by following rules. It's normal to return the fourth-best card of partner's suit, yes, but there are exceptions. For example, East could have done better on this deal:

```
North-South Vul.        ♠ 5
Dealer South            ♡ A 8 5 2
                        ◊ K 10 9 8 6
                        ♣ Q 9 4
  ♠ A J 9 4                              ♠ K 10 7 3
  ♡ 10 7 6          ┌─────────┐          ♡ Q J 4
  ◊ J 4 2           │    N    │          ◊ 7 3
  ♣ A 10 8          │  W   E  │          ♣ 7 6 5 2
                    │    S    │
                    └─────────┘
                        ♠ Q 8 6 2
                        ♡ K 9 3
                        ◊ A Q 5
                        ♣ K J 3
```

WEST	NORTH	EAST	SOUTH
			1NT
pass	2♣	pass	2♠
pass	3NT	all pass	

West had a difficult lead to make. He knew from the Stayman bid that there would be four hearts in the dummy. Since he was unimpressed by his holdings in the minor suits, he led the ♠4. Take the

East cards now. Your king wins the first trick. Which card will you return?

Let's suppose you mutter the rule about returning the fourth-best card and place the ♠3 on the table. Declarer will cover with the six and there will be no way to defeat the contract thereafter. When partner wins with the nine, he will not be able to continue the suit. Nor will he be any better placed when he gains the lead with the ace of clubs. The contract will be made.

To defeat the notrump game you need to score four spade tricks and one club trick. At Trick 2 you should lead the ten of spades, aiming to retain the lead if declarer chooses not to play a top card. As you see, returning the ten will guarantee the downfall of the contract. Such a play is often necessary when declarer holds four cards in the suit that has been led.

Another so-called rule is to play 'third hand high'. It is well known that you don't do this when you might promote a trick for the dummy:

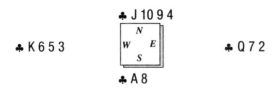

West leads the ♣6 against a notrump contract. If you play 'third hand high', contributing the king, declarer will score an undeserved second club trick. Instead you should put in the nine. In this particular position, the play works like a charm. The nine forces the ace and your king is still poised to prevent dummy's queen from scoring. Suppose instead that declarer held ♣J-5 or ♣10-5. Nothing would be lost! He would score one trick, yes, but that was guaranteed even if you played your king.

How many times do defenders go wrong in this situation?

```
            ♣ J 10 9 4
              ┌───────┐
              │   N   │
 ♣ K 6 5 3    │ W   E │    ♣ Q 7 2
              │   S   │
              └───────┘
            ♣ A 8
```

Partner leads the ♣3 and declarer plays the four from dummy. If you surrender the queen, you know what is likely to happen. Declarer will win with the ace or king and score three tricks in the suit. Play low instead and declarer will be held to just two club tricks. Indeed, if South started with ♣K-8 and has few entries to dummy, you may restrict him to just one club trick by playing low. Partner's ace can win the second round and your queen will win the third. (In a suit contract you might defend differently, to establish one quick trick in the suit.)

Another time to break the 'third hand high' notion is when the play of the lower of two honors will force out declarer's stopper in the suit, leaving communications fluid for the defense.

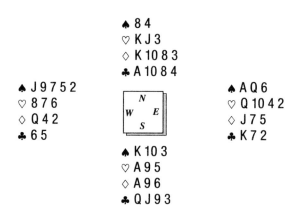

South plays in 3NT and West leads the ♠5. How should you plan the defense on the East cards? If you play the ace at Trick 1, the contract will be made. Declarer will hold up the spade king when you return the queen of the suit. After winning the third round of spades, he will take the club finesse. It loses but you have no spade to play.

A better idea is to play the queen of spades at Trick 1. Declarer can hardly risk a hold-up — if West has led from a holding such as ♠A-J-7-5-2, the defenders will claim five immediate spade tricks. He wins with the spade king and once again takes the club finesse. What a difference! When you win the club king you can run four spade tricks. One down.

When you judge that partner is likely to have led from a five-card suit, you might make the same play with A-J-x in the spade suit. It wouldn't matter too much if declarer scored an undeserved trick when holding queen third in spades. You would still get the contract one down when you came on lead in clubs. The real benefit would come when declarer held king third and, once again, you forced out his stopper on the first round.

Key points

1. When you return the suit that partner has led, play the top card from two remaining cards, otherwise the original fourth-best card. This will allow partner to judge whether he should win the second round or hold up a high card to maintain communications.

2. When you have bid a suit such as A-K-x-x-x, and partner subsequently leads the suit against a notrump contract, consider playing a low card to maintain contact with your partner.

3. When partner returns your lead with a middle card and declarer plays low, consider whether you can afford to overtake. This may be necessary when partner has no further card to play in the suit. In such a circumstance it may pay you to overtake even when this concedes a trick in the short term.

4. When playing high in the third seat may set up one of dummy's cards, think carefully before doing so. It is particularly wasteful to play a high card when declarer holds one or two honors bare, and will have to play high anyway.

A.

♠ 9 4
♡ K Q 6
◇ A J 7 3
♣ 10 8 5 3

♠5 led

```
      N
  W       E
      S
```

♠ A Q 6
♡ 10 8 4
◇ 10 9 6 3
♣ 9 7 2

South opens 1NT (15-17) and is raised to 3NT. Partner leads the
♠5 and you must consider how to play to the first trick. Do not
answer too quickly. What is the purpose behind the card that you
play?

B.

♠ K 10 5
♡ A J 2
◇ 8 6
♣ Q 9 8 5 4

◇3 led

```
      N
  W       E
      S
```

♠ A 8 6
♡ 10 8 4
◇ A 10 9 2
♣ 9 7 2

South opens 1NT (15-17) and is raised to 3NT. You win partner's
◇3 lead with the ace. What card will you return?

C.

♠ 7 5 2
♡ A J 2
◇ A 6
♣ K J 9 5 2

♠8 led

```
      N
  W       E
      S
```

♠ A Q J 9 6 4
♡ 10 8 4
◇ J 8 3
♣ 7

North opens 1♣, you overcall 1♠, and South bids 2◇. North
rebids 3♣ and South closes the auction with 3NT. Plan the
defense.

Answers

A. Did you play the queen? The purpose of such a play is to force out declarer's stopper so that when *you* subsequently gain the lead there will be a route to partner's hand. Here you have no possible card of re-entry and it is partner who is likely to gain the lead. You should therefore win the first trick with the ace and return the queen, making the lie of the suit clear to partner. If instead you play the queen, there is a risk that he may place South with the ace and switch elsewhere when he gains the lead.

B. You should return a normal fourth-best ◇2. None of the reasons for breaking the standard rule are present. You may assume that partner has four diamonds. Declarer therefore has only three and there is no need to hold the lead in order to play a third round from your side. Neither can the suit become blocked, which is possible only when partner holds five cards in the suit led.

C. You must hope that partner has a doubleton spade rather than a singleton. Play the jack on the first trick. Declarer will have to win with the king if the suit is distributed 2-3-6-2 round the table. Partner will then be able to reach your hand, should he gain the lead.

CHAPTER 4

Defense against Suit Contracts

Defending against a suit contract can be more difficult than defending against notrump, if only because you have a greater variety of tactics to consider. Should you play for a ruff? Should you try to set up winners before declarer can establish discards? Should you play trumps to reduce declarer's ruffs? Should you attack declarer's trump holding by playing on your own strongest suit? We addressed some of these questions in the chapter on opening leads and will deal with the technique of forcing declarer's trumps later in this chapter.

First, we will look at some important elements of technique which arise within a single suit. In particular, we will look at some mistakes that most players make hundreds of times throughout their bridge-playing careers. Avoid these errors in your own play and you will leap-frog over your rivals.

Playing the right card in the third seat

You will be familiar with the general guideline: play high in the third seat. Its purpose is to avoid a horror story in this type of position:

```
                        ◇ 9 7 6 2
                        ┌─────────┐
                        │    N    │
        ◇ Q 8 5 3       │ W     E │       ◇ K 10 4
                        │    S    │
                        └─────────┘
                        ◇ A J
```

Your partner leads the ◇3 against, say, a spade game. Of course you must put up the king. Partner's queen will then score on the second round. It is totally obvious to a sound player but you will still see defenders who are reluctant to expend such a valuable card. Amazing!

Many players go wrong here too, sad to say:

◇ 9 7 5

◇ Q J 10 8 4 3   ◇ A 6 2

◇ K

West leads the ◇Q and East plays low ('to force out the king, partner'). No longer needing to lose a diamond trick, declarer will laugh all the way to the bank.

The situation is less clear-cut when dummy has an honor:

◇ K 7 2

◇ J 9 8 3   ◇ A 10 4

◇ Q 6 5

Partner leads the ◇3 and declarer plays low from dummy. If you play the ace you promote dummy's king and declarer will score two tricks from the suit. By playing the ten, and keeping your ace to deal with dummy's king, you restrict declarer to one diamond trick. Partner would not have underled the queen and jack against a suit contract, so you know that declarer will win the first trick with the queen or jack. Your primary concern is to avoid giving him a further trick with dummy's king.

What about this situation?

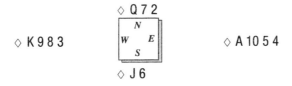

◇ Q 7 2

◇ K 9 8 3   ◇ A 10 5 4

◇ J 6

Your partner leads the ◇3. Defending in notrump, it would be automatic to insert the ten. You would do this to avoid conceding a second trick, should declarer hold K-x. You would also score four tricks in the suit when the lead was from such as K-J-8-3.

Defending a suit contract, there is no easy answer. Playing the ten will work well when partner has led from the jack, or from the king-jack. It may not work so well when he has led from the king. True, if you rise with the ace, declarer can establish a diamond trick eventually. By then, though, you might have been able to beat the contract by scoring (or establishing) tricks in the other suits. You must take your time in such a situation, looking at the other suits and calculating the prospects for beating the contract, one way or another.

Suppose, for example, that this is the full deal:

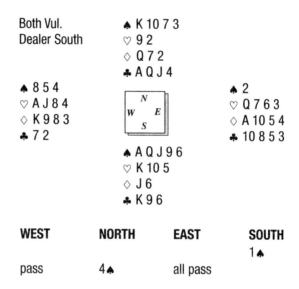

Both Vul.	♠ K 10 7 3		
Dealer South	♡ 9 2		
	◇ Q 7 2		
	♣ A Q J 4		

♠ 8 5 4
♡ A J 8 4
◇ K 9 8 3
♣ 7 2

♠ 2
♡ Q 7 6 3
◇ A 10 5 4
♣ 10 8 5 3

♠ A Q J 9 6
♡ K 10 5
◇ J 6
♣ K 9 6

WEST	NORTH	EAST	SOUTH
			1 ♠
pass	4 ♠	all pass	

Partner leads the ◇ 3 and declarer plays low from dummy. Unless the lead is from precisely ◇ K-J-3, you cannot take three diamond tricks. How can the contract be beaten if West does not have this somewhat unlikely holding?

There are two plausible routes to four tricks for the defense. The first is that you can score two diamond tricks and two heart tricks. To play for this chance, you must rise with the ace of diamonds and switch to a low heart (declarer may misguess if his hearts are headed by the king-jack). The other chance is that you can score three tricks in the red suits and one trump trick. In this case, too, you need to win with the ace of diamonds and switch to a low heart.

You see the thought processes involved? You must calculate which cards partner needs to beat the contract, then follow the defense most likely to succeed. On a different layout of the cards, you might be able to tell that only one trick could be scored outside the diamond suit. In that case you would play the ◊ 10 at Trick 1, hoping to score three tricks in diamonds.

Many players go wrong in this position:

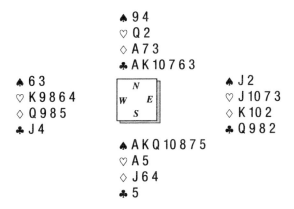

◊ Q 10 9
◊ J 8 6 2
◊ K 7 3
◊ A 5 4

Partner chooses the wrong moment to lead a diamond from jack fourth, against a trump contract, and the nine is played from dummy. How many times do you see defenders putting on the king? It is a bad mistake to make. Since West would not have underled an ace against a suit contract, South is known to hold that card. If East plays the king, declarer will be able to score three diamond tricks, finessing the ten on the second round. If East plays low, dummy's nine will win, yes, but declarer will be held to two tricks in the suit.

There are several other exceptions to the 'third hand high' rule. When partner has led a trump, and you are unlikely to score a trick in the suit, withholding your top card may kill an important entry to dummy. Take the East cards here:

♠ 9 4
♡ Q 2
◊ A 7 3
♣ A K 10 7 6 3

♠ 6 3
♡ K 9 8 6 4
◊ Q 9 8 5
♣ J 4

♠ J 2
♡ J 10 7 3
◊ K 10 2
♣ Q 9 8 2

♠ A K Q 10 8 7 5
♡ A 5
◊ J 6 4
♣ 5

South reaches a small slam in spades and your partner leads the three of trumps, declarer playing the four from dummy. No alarm bell will sound, but the fate of the contract hangs on your choice of card at Trick 1. Suppose you expend the jack. Declarer will win, cross to the ♣A, and ruff a club high. He will then cross to the nine of trumps (yes) and take another club ruff with a high trump. A diamond to the ace will provide access to the two established clubs and thirteen tricks will result.

It is pointless to play the jack on the first trick. Play low and declarer will not have enough entries to establish and reach the clubs. Twist and turn as he may, the slam will go one down.

Another time when it may be wrong to play high in the third seat is when doing so may set up several tricks for declarer. Suppose your partner leads the ♡9 against a diamond slam and this is the position you can see:

```
                        ♡ 7 5
                     ┌─────────┐
                     │    N    │
        ♡9 led       │ W     E │       ♡ K 8 6 4 2
                     │    S    │
                     └─────────┘
                     ♡ unknown
```

Declarer is marked with A-Q-J-10 in the heart suit and will score four heart tricks if you play the king. Playing low restricts him to three.

It can also be expensive to release an ace in the third seat :

```
Neither Vul.          ♠ K Q 9 5 4 3
Dealer South          ♡ 9
                      ◇ A 7 4
                      ♣ A J 10
♠ 7 2                ┌─────────┐      ♠ 8
♡ 8 4                │    N    │      ♡ A J 10 7 5 3 2
◇ K 9 6 3            │ W     E │      ◇ Q J 2
♣ 8 7 6 4 2          │    S    │      ♣ 9 3
                     └─────────┘
                      ♠ A J 10 6
                      ♡ K Q 6
                      ◇ 10 8 5
                      ♣ K Q 5
```

WEST	NORTH	EAST	SOUTH
			1NT (15-17)
pass	2♡ (transfer)	3♡	3♠
pass	4NT	pass	5◇
pass	6♠	all pass	

Partner leads the ♡8 in response to your overcall. Declarer covers with dummy's nine. How should you react?

There is room for partner to hold only one card of value. If this is the ♣K, declarer can finesse against it successfully. Your only real chance is that partner holds the ◇K. Let's see what happens if you release the ace of hearts at Trick 1. Declarer will win the return, draw trumps, and throw two of dummy's diamonds on the ♡KQ. That's no good. Suppose instead that you cover dummy's ♡9 with the ten. Declarer will not lose a heart trick now, but he will have two inescapable losers in diamonds! The heart ace will have been sacrificed in a worthy cause.

Playing the right card in second seat

What's the rationale behind the general guideline: Play low in the second seat? It's simply that you should not play high cards on thin air. Declarer will have to commit a high card himself anyway, in third seat, so it is usually a waste of time putting up a high card yourself. This is a basic situation (declarer is playing on a side suit in a trump contract):

More than once we have seen defenders putting up the king in the second seat. 'It was dead, anyway,' they inform their horrified partners. Of course the defenders would have scored a trick in the suit, if only West had played low on the first round.

Slightly more defenders go wrong in this situation:

◇ K 3

◇ A 10 8 5 2   W E   ◇ J 7 4

◇ Q 9 6

Declarer leads the six or nine of diamonds towards the dummy. If West climbs up with the ace he will concede two tricks in the suit.

This situation is similar. Take the West cards here:

♣ J 6 3

♣ Q 8 5 4   N / W E / S   ♣ K 9 2

♣ A 10 7

Declarer leads the ♣7 towards the dummy. If you are tempted to rise with the queen, declarer will finesse against partner's king on the next round and score two tricks in the suit. You should play low.

Sometimes you will have to steel yourself to play low from Q-x or K-x too! Suppose you are East and one of declarer's suits (perhaps the trump suit) lies like this:

♥ A Q 6 5 3

♥ J 10 8   N / W E / S   ♥ K 7

♥ 9 4 2

Declarer leads the ♥3 from dummy. If you rise with the king, declarer will lose only one trick in the suit. Play low, without giving the matter any apparent thought, and partner will win the first round. Declarer will doubtless finesse on the next round and your side will score two heart tricks.

Why do most players go in with the king? It must be because they fear that South has jack third. With that holding, however, he would surely have led low to the queen, hoping that West held a doubleton king.

What is your general reaction when declarer leads a side-suit singleton from the dummy and you are sitting in second position with the ace? Do you play it at the speed of light, muttering 'it's now or never'?

If you do, you are in good company. However, such a play is usually wrong. Suppose the side suit lies like this:

♦ 5

♦ Q 10 7 4   N / W E / S   ♦ A 9 8 3

♦ K J 6 2

When you rise with the ace you save declarer a guess in the suit. If you duck smoothly, he may underestimate you and conclude that you cannot hold the ace. He will finesse the jack, playing you for the queen, and not make a trick in the suit.

Perhaps the hidden hands lie differently:

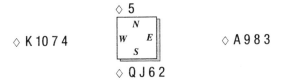

In this scenario, rising with the ace sets up a ruffing finesse against partner's king.

If you would like to see a whole-deal example of holding up an ace when a singleton is led through you, turn back three pages to the 6♠ contract in the previous section. Suppose that your partner leads a trump and this is won in the dummy. When declarer leads the ♡9 from dummy you must merely cover the card with the ten (or jack). As we saw when partner led a heart, it will cost the contract if you put up the ace.

Just about the only time that it is right to go in with the ace is when you can see (or have good expectations of) the setting tricks elsewhere.

Thinking clearly in defense

Much of the time, you can arrive at the best defense by sitting back in your chair and thinking clearly about the various possibilities. Does that sound easy? Sometimes it is, sometimes it isn't! Cover the East and South hands here and consider the defense from the West seat.

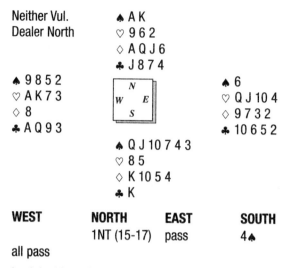

Neither Vul.
Dealer North

♠ A K
♡ 9 6 2
♢ A Q J 6
♣ J 8 7 4

♠ 9 8 5 2
♡ A K 7 3
♢ 8
♣ A Q 9 3

♠ 6
♡ Q J 10 4
♢ 9 7 3 2
♣ 10 6 5 2

♠ Q J 10 7 4 3
♡ 8 5
♢ K 10 5 4
♣ K

WEST	NORTH	EAST	SOUTH
	1NT (15-17)	pass	4♠
all pass			

You lead the king of hearts against South's spade game and partner plays the queen, telling you that he holds the jack also. How should you continue at Trick 2?

A low club would work well if declarer started with only one heart and partner held K-x of clubs. This is a very unlikely situation, however. Perhaps you should play a low heart to partner's jack. A club return will then beat the contract, provided declarer has at least two clubs.

If you opt for either of those choices, you have not been thinking as clearly as you might have. Try playing your singleton diamond! The trump suit is blocked so declarer will have to lead a plain suit from dummy after cashing the trump ace-king. If he plays a diamond, you will score your ruff immediately. If instead he plays a heart, partner will win and give you your diamond ruff. Declarer's only other play is a club. You will win with the ace and cross to partner's ♡J for a diamond ruff.

You may be wondering how partner knows that he should play a diamond back, rather than a club. Do you see the inference that he should draw? If you wanted a club back, you would have played a heart to the jack at Trick 2, rather than exiting with a diamond. Much good defense is like this. Not at all easy and you have to *think* to arrive at the right answer.

On the next deal, East had an apparent problem with his discarding. Thinking clearly would have provided the solution. Take the East cards and — if you're willing to risk it! — test your own mental processes.

North-South Vul.
Dealer South

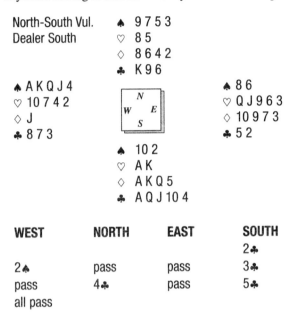

♠ 9 7 5 3
♡ 8 5
◇ 8 6 4 2
♣ K 9 6

♠ A K Q J 4
♡ 10 7 4 2
◇ J
♣ 8 7 3

♠ 8 6
♡ Q J 9 6 3
◇ 10 9 7 3
♣ 5 2

♠ 10 2
♡ A K
◇ A K Q 5
♣ A Q J 10 4

WEST	NORTH	EAST	SOUTH
			2♣
2♠	pass	pass	3♣
pass	4♣	pass	5♣
all pass			

West, your partner, opens the defense with three top spades. You throw a heart on the third round and declarer ruffs. Four rounds of trumps are played and you must find two more discards. Another heart can easily be spared but what next from ♡QJ9 ◇10973?

At the table East threw a diamond, retaining the more senior holding in hearts. Declarer scored four tricks in the diamond suit and the game was made. Can you see why East should have thrown a heart and kept the diamond guard instead?

The point that East missed was that South would have taken at least one heart ruff in dummy if he held more than two cards in the suit. Once East draws this inference, it is easy to see that there can be no point in keeping the heart guard.

General guidance on discarding

Choosing the right discards can be difficult at times. Ideally, you should attempt to match the length of your holdings with those of dummy and the declarer. Dummy's lengths are on display; those of declarer can often be deduced from the bidding or from partner's count signals.

Suppose you are sitting East and this is your view of one of declarer's side suits:

You should be reluctant to throw a club. If your partner has the queen, you are guarding the fourth round of the suit. If declarer happens to hold the queen, it will do you little good to throw a club and retain some guard elsewhere. When declarer plays his four club winners you will have to release the other guard anyway.

Be careful, too, with a side suit like this:

Throw a spade and declarer may score a trick with the fourth round of the suit. If he started with a doubleton spade, he can ruff the fourth card good. If instead he started with three cards in the suit, he can concede the third round and still set up a winner.

Sometimes you will have to throw away your potential guard in one suit or another. A valuable guide in this situation is 'retain the guard in the suit where you can actually see the threat.'

West had to bear this advice in mind when defending here:

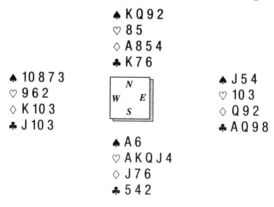

South arrived in 4♡ and West led the ♣J. Declarer played low from dummy (in case East held A-Q bare) and the defenders claimed three club tricks. East then continued with a fourth round of clubs, hoping to promote a trump trick for his partner. Declarer ruffed high, so West threw a diamond, as did dummy. After cashing dummy's ace of diamonds, declarer played off four rounds of trumps. On the last of these West had to find a discard from ♠10873 ◊K. What should he have done?

Thinking that declarer held the ◊Q, West threw a spade. Disaster! Declarer now claimed four spade tricks for his game. Why was West's defense wrong? It was quite possible that South held the ◊Q but in that case there would be no way to beat the contract. It was West's duty to defend the threat that he could actually see — the spades in dummy. South had to hold the spade ace or East would have cashed it at Trick 4.

Playing a forcing defense

When you hold four trumps in defense, or suspect that your partner does, it will frequently be right to direct your attack at declarer's trump holding. By leading your strongest suit, eventually forcing declarer to ruff, you may be able to gain trump supremacy. Let's see a full-deal example of this straight away.

Both Vul.	♠ K 10 7	
Dealer North	♡ J 4 2	
	◊ A 9 3	
	♣ A 7 6 4	

♠ A 8 5 3		♠ 2
♡ A 9	N	♡ 10 8 7 6 3
◊ K J 8 7 4	W E	◊ Q 10 5
♣ 10 5	S	♣ J 9 8 2

♠ Q J 9 6 4
♡ K Q 5
◊ 6 2
♣ K Q 3

WEST	NORTH	EAST	SOUTH
	1♣	pass	1♠
pass	1NT	pass	2♣ (checkback)
pass	2♠	pass	4♠
all pass			

Declarer may seem destined to lose only one diamond and the two major-suit aces. However, if you defend skillfully you can beat the game. To attack declarer's trump holding, you must lead your most powerful suit — diamonds. Declarer plays low from dummy and partner contributes to the cause by producing the diamond queen. His ◇ 10 return is won in the dummy and declarer plays the king of trumps. How will you defend?

Suppose you win with the ace and play another diamond. You will not beat the contract. Declarer will ruff, reducing himself to the same trump length as you. Instead of drawing trumps next, however, he will knock out the ace of hearts. A further attack in diamonds will be unproductive — there is still a trump in dummy and declarer will ruff the fourth round of diamonds there. He can then enter his hand with a club to draw your trumps and claim the contract.

Instead you should duck the first round of trumps and continue the good work by ducking the second round, too. This leaves declarer with two losing options. Suppose he switches his attention to hearts now. You will take the ace and force the South hand with a third round of diamonds, reducing declarer to the same number of trumps that you hold. When he eventually plays a third round of trumps, you will take your ace and force his last trump with a fourth diamond, ensuring a trick for your long trump.

If, instead, declarer plays a third round of trumps immediately, you will win and force his penultimate trump with a third round of diamonds. These cards will remain:

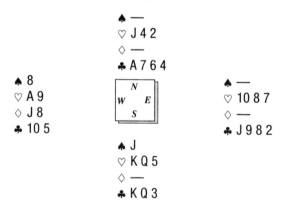

Declarer's best chance is to draw your last trump and to play on hearts, hoping that your partner holds the heart ace and has no more diamonds. He will go two down.

What were the two most important things to remember about this deal? First, you needed to attack in your strongest suit to put declarer's trumps under attack. Second, you had to hold up the ace of trumps until there were no more trumps in dummy. This ensured that any further diamonds would have to be ruffed in the South hand.

Key points

1. The general rule in the third seat is to play your highest card. Be wary of doing this when it will promote a high card in dummy. Be reluctant also to part with your highest trump, after a trump lead. This may provide declarer with an extra entry to dummy.

2. The general rule in the second seat is to play low. Even when you hold a doubleton king or queen and can see that this card will win the trick, you should be reluctant to play an honor on thin air. Doing so will often set up a second-round finesse against your partner.

3. When declarer leads a side-suit singleton from dummy, it is rarely right to go in with the ace in the second seat. There are several ways in which this may cost a trick.

4. When you hold four trumps, or suspect that partner may hold four trumps, it is often best defense to lead your strongest side suit. You hope to force declarer to ruff, thereby promoting your side's long trumps.

5. With a trump holding such as ace fourth, it is often important that you do not release the ace until one of the opposing hands plays its last trump. You can then win and attack the remaining trump length in the other hand.

A.

♠ K J 10 3
♡ 6 3
◇ A Q 9 6
♣ A 7 5

♡10 led

```
    N
W       E
    S
```

♠ A 7 6 4
♡ A K Q 2
◇ 10 4
♣ 10 8 3

North opens 1◇ and South arrives in 4♠ after the uncontested auction (1◇ - 1♠ - 2♠ - 3♣ - 4♠). Partner leads the ♡10. Plan the defense.

B.

♠ 9 7 4
♡ K Q 9 4
◇ A 10 8
♣ J 8 2

◇3 led

```
    N
W       E
    S
```

♠ J 10 6
♡ 8 3
◇ J 7 6 2
♣ A Q 6 4

After an auction of 1♡ - 3♡ - 4♡, partner leads the ◇3, covered by the ◇8. Do you play the jack? What is the purpose of your play?

C.

♠ A Q 9 2
♡ Q 9 4
◇ 3
♣ A 10 8 5 2

♡3 led

```
        N
   W        E
        S
```

♠ 10 8 6
♡ K 10 7 2
◇ A 7 6 2
♣ 6 3

South opens 1♠ and North responds 4◇ (a splinter bid, showing a diamond shortage). South bids Blackwood and arrives in six spades, partner leading the ♡3. How will you defend if declarer plays (a) the queen (b) the nine from dummy. What will your general plan be when declarer eventually leads the ◇3 from dummy?

Answers

A. The opponents' auction gives you hope that declarer may hold only four trumps. Play three rounds of hearts, even if the third round will concede a ruff-and-discard. This will force declarer to ruff, either in dummy or his own hand. Thereafter plan to win the third round of trumps (when either dummy's or declarer's trumps will be exhausted), and then lead another heart to force the last trump.

B. Partner will not have underled the king-queen against a suit contract, so declarer must hold one of those cards. If South holds the king, he will score three diamond tricks whatever you do. If he holds the queen, he will score three tricks if you put on the jack (by winning and finessing on the next round). Playing low restricts him to two tricks in the suit.

C. Partner will not have underled the heart ace but he may hold the jack of the suit. If declarer plays the heart queen from dummy, you will cover with the king. If instead he tries the nine, you will play the ten. Let's assume that either of these plays will force declarer's ace of hearts. When declarer eventually leads his singleton diamond from dummy, you should rise with the ace. You or your partner holds the setting trick in hearts, so it would not be a good moment to duck!

Counting

Do you think your defense would improve enormously if you could see all fifty-two cards? Of course it would! That's why skilled defenders devote so much time to reconstructing the hidden hands. Once they know how many cards each player has in each suit, and where the high cards lie, defending becomes much easier.

How can you get this information? Unfortunately it is not just a question of paying $29.95 to some company on the Internet and receiving the appropriate gadget. Instead you will have to work hard on every deal that you defend, counting distribution and counting points. It is no exaggeration to say that counting is the very essence of good defense. Because it seems like hard work, and they play bridge for enjoyment, most of the world's bridge players are not willing to make the effort of counting. If you are willing to go the extra mile, you can improve your results significantly. What's more, it is not as arduous as all that. Once you get into the habit it becomes automatic.

Counting distribution

How do you count declarer's hand? (In this context 'count' means to establish the shape of a hand, for example to determine that the suits are divided 5-1-2-5.) You begin with a rough idea from the bidding. Then, whenever any player shows out of a suit during the play, you update your picture. You adjust it also when you see distributional signals from partner. Usually you will have a good idea of the count of the hands by Trick 5 or 6.

Let's look at the next deal from West's viewpoint. We will see how he counts the hand and how it is then easy for him to determine the correct defense.

```
Neither Vul.            ♠ 10 7 2
Dealer South            ♡ J 10 9 2
                        ◊ Q 7
                        ♣ K Q J 9
  ♠ A J 8 4                              ♠ Q 6 5
  ♡ A Q 3            ┌─────────┐         ♡ 7 5
  ◊ J 10 5          │    N    │          ◊ 9 8 6 4 2
  ♣ 10 8 3          │ W     E │          ♣ 7 6 5
                    │    S    │
                     └─────────┘
                        ♠ K 9 3
                        ♡ K 8 6 4
                        ◊ A K 3
                        ♣ A 4 2
```

WEST	NORTH	EAST	SOUTH
			1NT (15-17)
pass	2♣	pass	2♡
pass	4♡	all pass	

You lead the ◊J against South's heart game and dummy's queen wins the trick. The jack of trumps is run to your queen and you must now plan the remainder of the defense.

You can see two trump tricks and must therefore hope for two further tricks in the black suits to beat the game. You have a decision to make (either now, or — if you exit passively — later when you win the ace of trumps). Should you switch to spades, hoping that partner holds the spade king? Or should you exit in one of the other suits, waiting for two spade tricks to come to you later?

To come up with the right answer, you will need to count declarer's hand. A well-tutored partner will have given you a count on the diamond suit at Trick 1. On this layout he will have signaled an odd number of diamonds by following with his lowest card — the two. Declarer is unlikely to have opened 1NT when 4-5 in the red suits. He must hold three diamonds and therefore seven cards in the red suits. It follows that he has six black-suit cards. However these are divided between spades and clubs, declarer will have two spades left after cashing the clubs! So, you do not need to risk a spade switch.

Suppose instead that the cards lie like this:

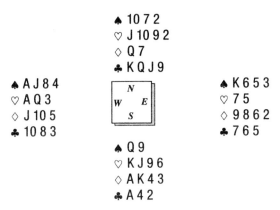

```
              ♠ 10 7 2
              ♡ J 10 9 2
              ◇ Q 7
              ♣ K Q J 9
♠ A J 8 4                        ♠ K 6 5 3
♡ A Q 3         N                ♡ 7 5
◇ J 10 5    W       E            ◇ 9 8 6 2
♣ 10 8 3        S                ♣ 7 6 5
              ♠ Q 9
              ♡ K J 9 6
              ◇ A K 4 3
              ♣ A 4 2
```

Now passive defense will allow declarer to throw a spade on the clubs. How can you tell this? Partner will signal with the ◇8 at Trick 1, showing four diamonds. Since this leaves declarer with only five black cards, you can tell that a passive defense will surrender the game. Whether South holds three spades and two clubs, or two spades and three clubs, he would lose only one spade.

You can see, from this one illustration, how important it can be to count the hand. Test yourself with the West cards here:

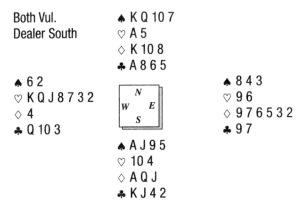

```
Both Vul.         ♠ K Q 10 7
Dealer South      ♡ A 5
                  ◇ K 10 8
                  ♣ A 8 6 5
♠ 6 2                                ♠ 8 4 3
♡ K Q J 8 7 3 2       N              ♡ 9 6
◇ 4               W       E          ◇ 9 7 6 5 3 2
♣ Q 10 3              S              ♣ 9 7
                  ♠ A J 9 5
                  ♡ 10 4
                  ◇ A Q J
                  ♣ K J 4 2
```

WEST	NORTH	EAST	SOUTH
			1NT (15-17)
2♡	3♡	pass	3♠
pass	6♠	all pass	

You lead the ♡K against the spade slam and dummy's ace wins. After drawing trumps in three rounds, declarer cashes the king and ace of diamonds and throws you in with the ♡10. What should you do?

Most defenders would count only the heart suit. It started as 7-2-2-2 around the table, so a heart return will give a ruff-and-discard. Ending their calculations at this point, they would play back a club in the hope that East held the jack. Declarer would then claim the remaining tricks.

Instead you should calculate declarer's shape. He started with four spades and two hearts. Your partner will have signaled high-low in diamonds, to show an even number. Since South would not open 1NT with 4-2-5-2 shape, he must hold three diamonds and therefore four clubs. It follows that it is safe to concede a ruff-and-discard when you gain the lead in hearts. Declarer will throw the fourth club from one hand or another but you will still score your ♣Q.

Counting points

As well as counting distribution, it can be important to count declarer's high-card points. Why should that be useful? Because it will let you know how many points partner holds. To see how this might be of benefit, suppose that the bidding and the appearance of the dummy tell you that partner cannot hold more than two points. You can steer clear of any defense that requires him to hold the ♡K!

Here is a deal where East's best defense can be determined by counting points. Take the East cards yourself.

```
Both Vul.              ♠ A 10 9 4
Dealer South           ♡ 6 5 4
                       ◇ A Q 6
                       ♣ 9 7 2
   ♠ 6 5 2                              ♠ K 7 3
   ♡ Q J 10 9 8        ┌─────────┐      ♡ K 2
   ◇ 7 5 3             │   N     │      ◇ K 8 4
   ♣ J 6              W│       E │      ♣ Q 10 8 4 3
                       │   S     │
                       └─────────┘
                       ♠ Q J 8
                       ♡ A 7 3
                       ◇ J 10 9 2
                       ♣ A K 5
```

WEST	NORTH	EAST	SOUTH
			1NT (15-17)
pass	3NT	all pass	

Seeing no benefit to using Stayman when his shape is 4-3-3-3, North raises directly to 3NT. Your partner leads the ♡Q and you overtake with the king to untangle the suit. Declarer allows your king to win and you must decide what to return at Trick 2. Any ideas?

Most defenders would return their remaining heart without further calculation. Declarer would win with the ace and set up his tricks in spades and diamonds, the finesses running into the safe East hand. Nine tricks would result.

Let's try again with those East cards, this time making an effort to reconstruct the hidden hands. How many points are on view between the East hand and dummy? Twenty-one. South has 15-17 points, so that leaves 2-4 points for West. He has already indicated three points in hearts, so he will have at most one jack outside hearts.

It is pointless to set up the hearts; partner will have no entry to enjoy them. Instead you should switch to a low club, hoping that partner holds the ♣J. Declarer will win with the ace and finesse in spades or diamonds. You win with the king and fire back the queen of clubs (to prevent declarer ducking the trick to partner's bare jack, if he has not already unblocked that card). The contract will now go two down — when declarer's second finesse fails, you will cash your established clubs.

Counting declarer's tricks

You may think that counting is not very glamorous stuff and you would rather see if there is something good on TV. The chapter is nearly through, so stay with us. The final type of counting we will discuss is that of declarer's tricks. On the next deal, this will guide you towards a dashing defensive move.

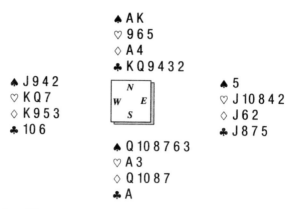

```
                    ♠ A K
                    ♡ 9 6 5
                    ◇ A 4
                    ♣ K Q 9 4 3 2
     ♠ J 9 4 2      ┌─────────┐      ♠ 5
     ♡ K Q 7        │    N    │      ♡ J 10 8 4 2
     ◇ K 9 5 3      │ W     E │      ◇ J 6 2
     ♣ 10 6         │    S    │      ♣ J 8 7 5
                    └─────────┘
                    ♠ Q 10 8 7 6 3
                    ♡ A 3
                    ◇ Q 10 8 7
                    ♣ A
```

Sitting West, you lead the ♡K against South's contract of six spades. Declarer wins with the ace, cashes the ace of clubs, and draws two rounds of trumps with the ace and king.

After the usual 'What have I done to deserve a trump break like that?' shake of the head, he throws a heart on the king of clubs and returns to his hand by ruffing a low club. How should you react in the West seat? Will you overruff or not?

Suppose you keep your trump length intact and throw a heart. What will happen? Count the tricks that declarer will make. He will play queen and another trump, giving you the lead. Whatever you return, declarer will now score five trump tricks, two red aces, and five club tricks. A total of twelve! That's no good.

Suppose instead that you overruff on the third round of clubs. If you exit passively with a second round of hearts, declarer will ruff, draw your last trump and score the same twelve tricks. How do you know that declarer will ruff the next heart? Firstly, your partner will have given you a length signal at Trick 1, telling you that South started with an even number of hearts. Secondly, if South began with three hearts he would surely have played a third high club, throwing his last heart loser.

So, what else can you try after overruffing the club? You must return the king of diamonds, forcing out dummy's ace! Declarer will then have no entry to dummy's club winners. The best he can do is to win with the diamond ace and finesse the ◇10. That move will be successful but you will still score the ◇9 on the fourth round of the suit. The ◇K switch — known as a Merrimac Coup — was risky and could be justified only because you could count declarer for twelve tricks on any other defense.

Are you ready for the last deal in the book? The West cards are yours, once again.

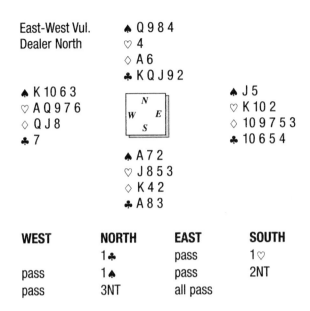

East-West Vul.
Dealer North

♠ Q 9 8 4
♡ 4
♢ A 6
♣ K Q J 9 2

♠ K 10 6 3
♡ A Q 9 7 6
♢ Q J 8
♣ 7

♠ J 5
♡ K 10 2
♢ 10 9 7 5 3
♣ 10 6 5 4

♠ A 7 2
♡ J 8 5 3
♢ K 4 2
♣ A 8 3

WEST	NORTH	EAST	SOUTH
	1♣	pass	1♡
pass	1♠	pass	2NT
pass	3NT	all pass	

With both majors bid by the opponents, you try your luck with the queen of diamonds. Declarer wins with the king and leads the ♠2. How will you defend?

Who holds the ace of clubs, do you think? Whenever declarer fails to attack a suit such as dummy's clubs here, it is a safe assumption that he holds the missing high card in the suit and that the tricks are ready to run. So, let's count declarer's tricks. He has five club tricks, you assume, and the two top cards in diamonds. If he has the ace of spades too, and you duck the spade king, the queen will score in dummy and he will claim nine tricks! If South has the spade ace, then, it is essential to rise with the spade king and switch to hearts, hoping to score the setting tricks in that suit. What is more, a count of declarer's points (♠A, ♢K, ♣A) will mark your partner with the ♡K.

What if East has the ♠A and declarer has the ♡K and ♠J? The same defense will still work! You will knock out South's ♡K, bringing his total to only eight tricks, and then have the best possible chance of running the rest of the heart suit when East gains the lead in spades.

Key points

1. The basis of most good defense is counting. A good defender will count distribution, points and tricks.

2. As a defender, you have three main sources of information about the distribution. The opponents' bidding may reveal their length in one or more suits. Every time one of the closed hands shows out of a suit, you will have a complete count on it. Your partner will also give you count signals, showing whether he holds an odd or even number of cards in the suit.

3. Sometimes you need partner to hold a particular card, or distribution, to beat the contract. If such a holding is possible on the information gathered so far, defend on the assumption that partner does indeed have that holding.

4. By counting declarer's tricks, you can sometimes tell that the original defense will not be quick enough. In that case you may be able to switch elsewhere, hoping that partner has a key card in the new suit.

A.

         ♠ J 9 7 2
         ♡ A 8 4
         ◇ K 7
         ♣ K 9 5 4

♠ Q 8 3
♡ J 10 9 2
◇ J 8 3
♣ Q 10 2

	N	
W		E
	S	

WEST	NORTH	EAST	SOUTH
			1♠
pass	4♠	pass	6♠
all pass			

Declarer wins your ♡J lead with the king and draws two rounds of trumps, partner showing out on the second round. He then crosses to the ♡A and ruffs a heart. Next come the king and ace of diamonds, partner signaling high-low. Declarer then throws you in with the trump queen. What will you do now?

B.

Suppose you hold the same West cards as in the first problem and the bidding goes the same way. This time, declarer wins the heart lead with the king, plays two rounds of trumps, and continues with the ace and queen of hearts. He cashes the king and ace of diamonds, then throws you in with the trump queen. How will you exit?

C.

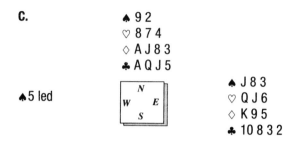

♠ 9 2
♡ 8 7 4
◇ A J 8 3
♣ A Q J 5

♠J 8 3
♡ Q J 6
◇ K 9 5
♣ 10 8 3 2

♠5 led

South opens a 15-17 1NT and North raises to game. Partner leads the ♠5 to the jack and ace. The ◇Q is run to your king. What now?

Answers

A. You must count declarer's shape. He started with five spades and two hearts. Partner high-low in diamond marks declarer with either four diamonds or two. If he held 5-2-4-2 shape he would simply have ruffed his two diamonds, so his shape must be 5-2-2-4. In this case, a ruff-and-discard will not assist him. You should exit with a fourth round of hearts. A club would surrender the contract if South held ♣A-J-x-x.

B. Declarer has shown up with three hearts this time, so his shape must be 5-3-2-3. A ruff-and-discard now would allow him to ruff in the dummy and discard the third club from the South hand. Since you can tell that this defense would give declarer the contract, you must switch to clubs, hoping that your partner holds the jack.

C. Is it possible that declarer started with A-x-x in spades and the ace-king of hearts? Surely not — with those cards he would have held up the spade ace until the third round. It looks as if South must hold the ace and king of spades. (Yes, he could have made life more difficult for you by winning with the king. Not all declarers know that!) If you play another spade and declarer wins, how many tricks will he have? Five in the majors and surely another four from the club suit. Is it possible for a heart switch to beat the contract? Yes, declarer's hand could be something like:

♠ A K 7 4   ♡ K 5 3   ◇ Q 10 4   ♣ K 6 5

You should switch to the ♡Q.

Just Published by Master Point Press

Win the Bermuda Bowl with Me
by Jeff Meckstroth and Marc Smith

"Unless you've actually done it, it's impossible to understand what it feels like to play in the Bermuda Bowl – that is, until now." — Zia Mahmood

"This is a book people will still want to read many years from now!" — Paul Soloway

"Jeff explains the game as well as he plays it. Need I say more?" — Larry Cohen, author of *To Bid or not to Bid*

Samurai Bridge
by Robert MacKinnon

Romance, adventure, swordplay — and plenty of bridge! This novel is *Seven Samurai* as Charles Goren might have written it!